La

Lady T's Etiquette Series

100 Do's and Don'ts of Social and Professional Etiquette

Published by
UrbanGirlz Incorporated
P.O. Box 3641, Cedar Hill, Texas 75106
www.urbangirlz.org

ISBN 10: 1466438029
ISBN 13: 978-1466438026

TEEN/YOUNG ADULT EDUCATION

Library of Congress Cataloging-In-Publication Data is available from the publisher.

This book is available for bulk discounts. For more information contact: ladyt@urbangirlz.org or call 1.800.291.6492.

Trenette Wilson

Lady T's Etiquette Series

Dedication

This book is dedicated to anyone who has ever been confused about which fork to use.

Lady T's Etiquette Series
Acknowledgments

I would like to thank my Lord and Savior, Jesus Christ. I would also like to thank my husband who is my greatest supporter and investor; I could not be a writer without you. I would also like to thank my children, grandchildren and mother for being such an encouragement and support for me throughout the writing process. Also, thank you to my family and friends for your prayers.

Finally, thank you to Miriam Glover, my public relations guru. This series would not have been a success without your guidance, and Amanii Wilson for challenging me to take this resource to the next level.

Cover Design
Trenette Wilson – Lady T
Landa Morgan – Nfuxion Designs

Photography
Daniel Smiley

Editing
Mavis Caldwell

Trenette Wilson

Lady T's Etiquette Series

Table of Contents

Lady T's Etiquette Series

Hello. I am so excited you decided to read this book. My name is Lady Trenette Wilson, better known to the world as "Lady T."

This is the first book in my new Lady T's Etiquette Series, which uncovers the secrets of etiquette and decorum in both a professional and personal environment.

The term "etiquette," according to Webster's Dictionary means, "ticket." Today, too many underserved children and youth are locked out of the doors of opportunity because they don't posses the ticket.

This resource is designed to introduce you to etiquette in both business and personal settings. From how to dine properly, to making a stellar first impression, Lady T's Etiquette Series will help you enhance both your professional and personal graces.

The need for you to know etiquette is crucial because business executives, as well as mid level managers are taught how to carry themselves, how to appropriately address others and how to succeed in an increasingly competitive world.

Being equipped with the basic rules of etiquette will prepare you to successfully navigate a corporate luncheon, or a difficult business meeting.

Reading this book will assist you as you embrace the next level of your career and life.

Lady T's Etiquette Series

Dining Etiquette

Lady T's Etiquette Series

Dining Etiquette

Lady T's Etiquette Series

1 **Dining Etiquette**

"Good food ends with good talk."

Geoffrey Neighbor

Recently, while dining out with my children, I had the distinct honor of sitting next to a couple of teens who were out on a date. At first, I wasn't really paying attention to them until out of nowhere a piece of bread grazed my head. As I looked up to see where it came from, I noticed the teens sitting quietly trying desperately to hold in their laughter.

"How rude," I lamented returning to my dinner. This incident and many other disturbing dining encounters prompted me to write this book.

After speaking to many of my children's peers, and discussing it with my clients, I determined, families don't eat together as much any more due to busy schedules; therefore, the dining skills that once were taught around the dinner table are no longer being taught.

This section offers timeless etiquette tips that will help even the messiest eater seem refined. From how to tip, to where to leave the napkin, learn the tools that will help you become a dining pro and avoid accidentally launching food into someone else's plate.

Dining Etiquette

1. **When dining out, do tip the server at least 15% of the bill.**
   Servers have to divide their tips with other restaurant workers and get paid a minimal hourly wage.

2. **Do leave your napkin in the chair or on the arm of the chair when you must excuse yourself from the table but will be returning.**
   This is a signal to the waiter that you will be back otherwise he/she may clear your plate.

3. **Don't season your food before you taste.**
   It could offend the cook or ruin a great tasting dish.

4. **When eating steak, cut two or three slices at a time.**
   Cutting up the entire steak will cause the steak juices to run out and dry out the meat.

5. **When dining with a potential client or employer, don't blow your soup or chili nor crush crackers into your bowl.**

You could blow hot soup on him/her and crackers make a mess and could become a distraction.

6. **Knives and spoons are on the right, forks and napkins are on the left.**
   You should know this to avoid using someone else's utensils.

7. **When at a buffet, don't overload your plate. Getting a reasonable amount of food and going back for seconds or thirds is perfectly acceptable.**
   A plate filled with too much food could spill.

8. **Don't talk loud during dinner and keep your voice down when talking on your cell phone.**
   Sometimes you don't realize how loud you are speaking, and your conversation can be overheard by other dinner guests.

9. **Don't throw your napkin in your plate or push your chair back when finished eating.**
   It makes you appear arrogant and unrefined.

10. **If wine is being served and you are not having any, to refuse, place your finger-tips lightly on the rim of the glass when the server approaches.**
    Don't turn the glass upside down.

11. **During a business dinner, take small bites.**
    This will give you time to respond if asked a question without having to chew up a mouth full of food.

12. **If you use sugar packages, stack and place them on the left side of the plate, tucked under the plate a bit.**
    This will help you hide them discretely.

13. Large dinner napkins should be placed on your lap in a rectangle. Smaller napkins can be completely unfolded.

Your napkin should be easy to retrieve and used to dab both sides of your mouth.

14. If you are an invited dinner guest, ask the host what they suggest instead of ordering the most expensive item on the menu.

Be considerate when invited to dinner and follow the lead of the host/hostess.

15. If you are hosting a dinner party, send out your invitations two weeks early.

Give people ample time to plan for a great evening.

16. When invited to a dinner party, it is courteous to bring a gift for the hostess as a demonstration of appreciation.

Never arrive to a dinner party empty handed.

17. Don't dominate the conversation during dinner.

All dinner guests want to share in the conversation.

18. When paying the dinner bill, don't point out its amount. Pay it discretely.

Complaining about the bill or passing it around for everyone to see makes guests uncomfortable and it makes you seem cheap.

19. Prepare to leave approximately thirty minutes after dinner is complete.

You don't want to wear out your welcome.

20. If you're in a buffet line, allow older people to fix their plates first.
Older people are due respect and often suffer from health problems, which makes it difficult for them to stand for long periods of time.

Bonus

21. When dining at home, relax and throw the other rules out of the window.
Relax and enjoy your meal in private.

Lady T's Final Thoughts...

Remember, closing big business deals often happen while dining. Be on your best behavior and remember business meals are not about eating.

Lady T's 100 Etiquette Tips

My Dining Etiquette Experience

_____

_____

_____

_____

My Dining Etiquette Strengths

_____

_____

_____

_____

My Dining Etiquette Weaknesses

_____

_____

_____

_____

_____

Trenette Wilson

Developing My Dining Etiquette Skills

_____

_____

_____

_____

_____

_____

_____

_____

_____

_____

_____

_____

_____

_____

_____

_____

_____

Lady T's Etiquette Series

Image Etiquette

Trenette Wilson

Lady T's Etiquette Series
Image Etiquette

Lady T's Etiquette Series

2 Image Etiquette

"Behavior is the mirror in which everyone shows their image."

Johann Wolfgang von Goethe

Though you can't read a book by its cover, you can tell a lot about what it's about by the way it is packaged. The same can be said about your image. You image is the message you send others about who you are. Your image includes your poise, grace, grooming, appearance and attitude.

Your image is your business card, and you should take time to make sure your image is polished daily.

55% of a person's perception about you begins with your appearance. Though it's not always fair to determine what you feel or think about someone based on their appearance, the truth is, people who take time to polish their look are more respected and successful.

This section provides tips that will help you add timeless pieces to your wardrobe and help you make a lasting first impression.

Image Etiquette

1. **Do build clothing clusters to diversify your wardrobe.**
   This includes foundational items mixed with non-traditional accessories.

2. **Do mix different prints with solids.**
   Prints soften the appearance of solids.

3. **Wearing a medium to dark solid colored and subtly patterned suite will make you appear slimmer.**
   Dark colors make you look smaller.

4. **Vertical stripes make you look slimmer and taller. The smaller the stripe the more business you look, the larger the stripe the more casual you look.**
   Vertical lines cause the eye to follow the pattern down, which elongates you.

5. **Horizontal lines make you look larger.**
   They cause the eye to follow the lines around your body.

6. **Fabrics that have shine or texture make you appear larger.**

Because of the reflection, it adds dimension to your body making you appear larger.

7. **If you're short, don't wear shoes that strap up your leg, it cuts them off visually.**
   Don't cut your leg in half with the wrong shoe.

8. **Do wear clothes that fit properly, and don't restrict movement.**
   When your clothes don't fit properly, you look un-kept and in a business setting, unprofessional.

9. **If you have an upcoming event, start shopping early so you won't have to spend more money on a piece of clothing you may not really want.**
   Waiting until the last minute always costs you more.

10. **If you have a big chest, wear jackets that extend to the hip to distract from your bust line.**
    Short jackets draw attention to your bust line and waistline.

11. **Do wear one color or tone of one color to help you appear slimmer.**
    When you wear one color, it creates a visual illusion of one slim line.

12. **Your attitude is a vital part of your "image."**
    Take care to have a good attitude at all times.

13. **Buy your foundation and core wardrobe items (suites, skirts, jackets and pants) in the best quality you can**

afford and mix with cheaper items.
Quality clothes last longer and fit better.

14. **Do blend the color of the hosiery, hem and shoes to make you appear taller.**
Stark color changes visually cuts you off.

15. **Do wear dark colors at the bottom to make your hips appear smaller. If you have a small bottom and you want it to appear larger, wear bright colors at the bottom.**
Dark colors move inward and light colors move outward.

16. **Tapered sleeves makes a woman look slimmer and taller.**
All tapered clothes slim you.

17. **Do buy more solids than prints.**
Prints go out of season quickly so use them to mainly enhance your wardrobe.

18. **Do exercise and remain active.**
Doing so will help you feel better, help your clothes fit better and increase your self-esteem.

19. **Don't carry a purse and briefcase at the same time.**
You don't want to be fumbling with too much.

20. **Do add a rhinestone to your hair to make your outfit more formal.**
The small sparkly details give you a touch of elegance.

Bonus

21. **Do use a light scent after showering while your skin is still wet to lock in a pleasant body odor.**
A faint pleasant scent will help you exude a sweet fragrance.

Lady T's Final Thoughts...

If you only get one chance to make a first impression, be sure it is one that you control and truly represents you.

My Image Etiquette Experience

_____

_____

_____

My Image Etiquette Strengths

_____

_____

_____

My Image Etiquette Weaknesses

_____

_____

_____

Developing My Image Etiquette Skills

_____

_____

_____

_____

_____

_____

_____

_____

_____

_____

_____

_____

_____

_____

_____

_____

_____

_____

Lady T's Etiquette Series

Business Etiquette

Business Etiquette

3

Lady T's Etiquette Series

3 Business Etiquette

*"Missing work gives your company the opportunity
to do your job without you.
Lady T*

From board room meetings to emailing potential clients, how you conduct yourself and interact with others in a business environment impacts the bottom line.

With unemployment at an all time high and job creation and retention low, learning the unspoken rules of business etiquette will improve your chances of moving rapidly up the corporate ladder.

My first job was in a corporate environment, which required professional attire. I was blessed to grow up around fierce women like my mother and her good friends who always had a power suite and pair of pumps in their closet.

In a business environment, I quickly found out the reason for such attention to detail. How you present yourself determines your progress in the company and in your career.

Learn how to avoid common etiquette mistakes made in a business environment, avoid social media faux pas and learn to greet clients with professionalism.

Business Etiquette

1. **Do arrive to work and to appointments at least five minutes early and make sure you are prepared.**
   It demonstrates your professionalism.

2. **Do return phone calls and e-mails within 24 hours.**
   You could destroy a wonderful relationship by not responding in a timely manner.

3. **Keep your personal work area clean and organized.**
   It speaks volumes about your attention to detail.

4. **Don't tell vulgar, racist or cruel jokes in the workplace.**
   It could offend others and threaten your job.

5. **Do turn your cell phone off during meetings.**
   Give your client or colleague your undivided attention.

6. **Do make every effort to go to work daily.**
   When you're absent, you give the company an opportunity to learn to do your job without you.

7. **Do assist on extra projects.**
   It demonstrates your teamwork skills and willingness to put personal ambitions aside for collective success.

8. **If in doubt, do the right thing.**
   Character and integrity are very important in business and in life.

9. **In business settings, introductions are based on rank.**
   Positions and titles are highly regarded in business.

10. **Do complete your assignments in a timely manner. If you foresee a problem, discuss it with the person who gave you the assignment.**
    Missing deadlines is a major error in the workplace. Don't procrastinate, get busy.

11. **Don't visit Facebook or inappropriate websites on your work computer. Companies regularly monitor employees' computer use.**
    If caught clicking on the wrong thing, you could be reprimanded or worse, fired.

12. The proper hand shake starts and stops crisply.
Be sure to make eye contact and don't hold the other person's hand too firmly.

13. In the workplace, less is more... keep the sparkle and glitz to a minimum.
You want colleagues to talk about your thoughts and work ethic, not your over-the-top attire. In more casual work environments, workplace attire can be more relaxed, check the corporate handbook.

14. During an introduction you should keep your response brief and friendly.
Value other's time. You don't want to appear insensitive by going on and on.

15. Do remember, even if you are on a first name basis with your supervisor, he/she is not your personal friend.
Always keep it professional.

16. In the business world, the only physical contact you should have with clients, customers and colleagues is a "handshake."
Many companies adhere to this rule to avoid sexual harassment litigation.

17. When writing a business email, spell out all abbreviations. Ex. w/; with.

Following this rule will help you when doing business in a global market where standard American abbreviations may not be used.

18. **After a call, if you have promised to get someone information, get it to them promptly.**
Honoring your word will build confidence and respect for your work.

19. **If your company has a dress code, be sure to follow it. If they don't, observe senior managers and dress in line with them.**
Your appearance is very important in a business environment.

20. **During a business meeting, think before you speak. If you disagree with something, disagree with respect.**
Your colleagues will appreciate your candor and ability to articulate your opinion in a respectful and helpful way.

Bonus

21. **Do check your work!**
Mistakes in emails or in correspondence weaken the credibility of your company.

Lady T's Final Thoughts…

Possessing strong **Business Etiquette** skills will enhance your career and allow you to build respect and trust among your colleagues.

Trenette Wilson

My Business Etiquette Experience

_____

_____

_____

My Business Etiquette Strengths

_____

_____

_____

My Business Etiquette Weaknesses

_____

_____

_____

Developing My Business Etiquette Skills

Trenette Wilson

Lady T's Etiquette Series

International Etiquette

Lady T's Etiquette Series

International Etiquette

Lady T's Etiquette Series

4 International Etiquette

*All major religious traditions carry basically the same message,
that of love, compassion and forgiveness the important thing is they
should be part of our daily lives."*
Dalai Lama

Despite the beauty of many of the countries overseas,
Americans are viewed as arrogant in the eyes of many people
abroad. One way to break down the barriers and debunk
these beliefs is to learn about other cultures.

Learning the proper way to dine, dress and behave while
visiting another country will endear you to the locals and
demonstrate your respect for their heritage and life.

This section takes you on a journey around the world and
introduces you to the basic rules governing your behavior
while visiting a foreign country. From France to Japan,
learning other's customs and beliefs will help you enjoy a
wonderful trip with great stories to tell and fabulous
shopping finds.

Remember when preparing to travel, research your
destination online and find out about the countries customs
and dress code. It would also be wise to map your trip so
you will not be in the wrong place at the wrong time.
Learning the customs of the locals will guarantee a great trip.

International Etiquette

1. **In most of the Middle East, it's bad manners for an outsider to discuss politics or religion.**
   Though freedom of speech is revered in the U.S., it is better not to be so expressive when abroad.

2. **The work week in most Muslim countries runs from Saturday to Wednesday or Thursday morning because prayers are said five times daily.**
   When planning a trip to a Muslim country, make sure to call ahead to arrange meetings on the appropriate day.

3. **Constant eye contact during a handshake is crucial in Mexico and Argentina.**
   When you can look a person in the eye, it builds trust.

4. **Do always be punctual in England.**
   Being late could cause you to lose business.

5. **In Japan, shoes should be easy to remove, as you will do so often.**
    Slip-ons are the best choice.

6. **Soft handshakes are common across Africa.**
    Don't grip hands too tightly because it makes you appear aggressive.

7. **Handshakes in Italy are common for both sexes and may include grasping the arm with the other hand.**
    Italians are warm and more physically expressive.

8. **When doing business in Latin America, dress conservatively. Suites and ties for men, unrevealing business suites and long dresses for women.**
    Stay away from short, tight or too bright.

9. **Don't slap anyone's back in northern Europe.**
    It's perceived as aggressive.

10. **In Saudi Arabia, meetings normally start an hour late.**
    Saudi Arabia has a more laid back schedule.

11. **Tipping is typically 10% in Brazil.**
    Brazilian cafes and restaurants expect you to tip.

12. **The traditional toast in Mexico is Salud (Sal-UUD.**
    Learning local customs will help you avoid awkward situations.

13. It's rude to be on time to a dinner party in India, but don't be more than 30 minutes late.
Make sure you are clear about your arrival time.

14. Don't put your hands under the table while dining in France, Germany, or Austria.
It's considered rude.

15. In Islamic tradition, the right hand is considered the correct and polite hand to use for daily tasks such as eating, writing and greeting people.
Your left hand is considered "unclean."

16. When traveling to another country, take some time to learn some polite phases in the local language.
It will endear you to the locals.

17. In European countries, do say "thank you" and "please" often.
Respecting local traditions will demonstrate your respect for their customs.

18. In Japan, if you are greeted with a bow return with a bow as low as the one you received.
Follow the lead of your host or hostess.

19. No business is done on Friday in Egypt. It's considered a holy day.
Religion is extremely important in Middle Eastern countries.

20. In Japan, women should not wear pants in a business situation.
It's considered offensive.

Bonus

21. Elderly Latinos should not be addressed using their first names.
In the Latino community, older people are treated with great respect.

Lady T's Final Thoughts...

International Etiquette boils down to **RESPECT**. Respecting the beliefs and customs of others will help you become a savvy global citizen.

My Etiquette Journal

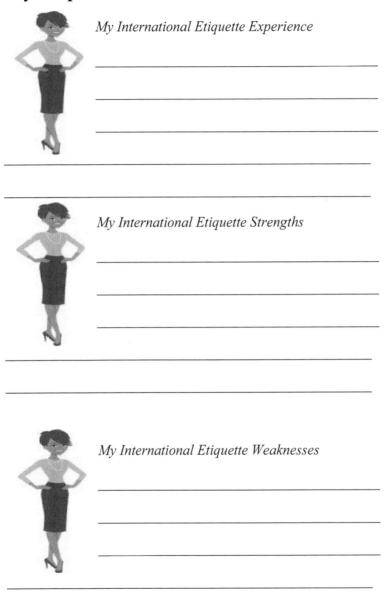

My International Etiquette Experience

_____

_____

_____

My International Etiquette Strengths

_____

_____

_____

My International Etiquette Weaknesses

_____

_____

_____

Developing My International Etiquette Skills

Lady T's Etiquette Series

Etiquette...for

Daily Living

Trenette Wilson

Lady T's Etiquette Series

Etiquette... for Daily Living

5

5 Etiquette...for Daily Living

"The world was my oyster, but I used the wrong fork."

Oscar Wild

The word "etiquette," means ticket. How fitting, as those who possess etiquette have doors opened for them while others who are not aware of proper decorum stay locked out of the door of progress.

Learning the rules of etiquette and implementing them in your daily life will help you seamlessly move in and out of social and business circles. Etiquette opens doors to opportunities both in the social and business world.

This section is designed to expose you to the common rules of decorum that are broken in everyday situations. From being at home, to shopping at the grocery store, there are rules of general etiquette that will help you appear poised and refined in all situations.

Learn basic rules of neighbor etiquette, disability etiquette and giving great gifts.

Etiquette...for Daily Living

1. **When giving a gift, stick to modesty and quality.**
   A small quality gift is better than a large cheap one.

2. **Do keep your dog on a leash and clean up after it.**
   Your neighbors will appreciate your thoughtfulness.

3. **When conducting a presentation, do adjust your speech to the audience being mindful of gender, religion or socio-economic background.**
   People cling on to your every word make sure they're not offensive.

4. **If someone buys you a gift (i.e. wedding, baby showers) send them a thank you card within one week of the gift.**
   It demonstrates your appreciation.

5. **When checking in your bags at an airport skycap, make sure to tip a minimum of a $1 to $2 per bag.**
   Despite the airlines new charges for carry-on bags, skycaps are not paid well and depend on the generosity of the public.

6. **Do help an elderly person across the street, open a door or carry their groceries.**
   Chivalry is not dead, it lives in you.

7. **Never point out how strange or different someone with a disability looks.**
   Always show respect for and to others.

8. **Be considerate when traveling, do warn the person behind you when you are about to recline your seat.**
   Airplanes seats are a tight fit, other passengers will appreciate your consideration.

9. **Do keep your property in order and clean and be sure to keep your belongings off your neighbor's yard.**
   There's nothing worse than a dirty neighbor.

10. **People who can't speak are referred to as "without speech."**
    Don't mistakenly refer to them slow or dumb.

11. **Taking pictures while visiting a museum is usually not permitted. Be sure to respect the rules.**
    Call ahead and find out their rules.

12. **When traveling, your clothes should mirror the residents of your destination.**
    Don't draw unwanted attention to yourself when abroad.

13. When traveling by sea, bring soft luggage.
Soft luggage is easier to store.

14. Avoid the words handicapped and crippled. The more respectful word is disabled.
Mocking or teasing people with disabilities is cruel.

15. If you borrow money, pay it back. If you can't pay it back when you said you would, let the person know.
Friendships are ruined because of unpaid debts.

16. Do pick up your trash when visiting a park.
Children and families want to enjoy the park too.

17. Do return something you borrow in a timely manner in the same or better condition than when you receive it.
Take care of things you have borrowed better than you would take care of your own things.

18. Do keep your trash in your yard and make sure your trash cans are clean and closed.
Dogs and cats tend to gather where unkept trash is.

19. Do call ahead if you plan on visiting someone.
Showing up at someone's house unannounced could lead to an unwelcomed reception.

20. Do say thank you if someone compliments you.
It doesn't cost anything to be polite.

Bonus

21. Avoid distractions when driving.

This will help you avoid accidents and road rage.

Lady T's Final Thoughts...

Etiquette for **Daily Living** really involves one thing. Do unto others as you would have them do unto you. Being kind and considerate to others is the highest form of etiquette.

Trenette Wilson

My Daily Etiquette Experience

_____

_____

_____

_____

My Daily Etiquette Strengths

_____

_____

_____

_____

My Daily Etiquette Weaknesses

_____

_____

_____

_____

_____

_____

Lady T's Etiquette Series

Lady T's Journal Pages

Use the following section to practice your etiquette skills daily.

Lady T's 100 Etiquette Tips

Monday – Practice on your Dining Skills

_____

_____

_____

_____

_____

_____

_____

_____

_____

_____

_____

_____

_____

_____

_____

_____

_____

_____

Trenette Wilson

Tuesday – Practice on your Image

_____

_____

_____

_____

_____

_____

_____

_____

_____

_____

_____

_____

_____

_____

_____

_____

_____

Lady T's 100 Etiquette Tips

Wednesday – Practice on your Business Skills

_____

_____

_____

_____

_____

_____

_____

_____

_____

_____

_____

_____

_____

_____

_____

_____

_____

Trenette Wilson

Thursday – Practice on your Public Speaking

_____

_____

_____

_____

_____

_____

_____

_____

_____

_____

_____

_____

_____

_____

_____

_____

_____

Lady T's 100 Etiquette Tips

Friday – Practice on Daily Etiquette

_____

_____

_____

_____

_____

_____

_____

_____

_____

_____

_____

_____

_____

_____

_____

_____

Trenette Wilson

Saturday - Results

Lady T's 100 Etiquette Tips

Sunday - Results

_____

_____

_____

_____

_____

_____

_____

_____

_____

_____

_____

_____

_____

_____

_____

_____

_____

Lady Trenette Wilson is the founder & CEO of NAUEP and the award winning online community www.urbangirlz.org, which is dedicated to educating, inspiring and celebrating urban girls and teens.

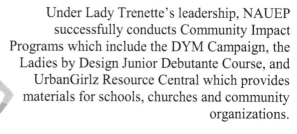

Under Lady Trenette's leadership, NAUEP successfully conducts Community Impact Programs which include the DYM Campaign, the Ladies by Design Junior Debutante Course, and UrbanGirlz Resource Central which provides materials for schools, churches and community organizations.

To contact Lady T - P.O. Box 3641, Cedar Hill, Texas 75106 or call 1.800.291.6492.

Lady T's Published Titles

Non-Fiction
10 Strategies of Successful Teenz
Lady T's Etiquette Series
Bible Basics Resource Guide
UrbanGirlz Guide to Etiquette Business
Ladies by Design Junior Debutante Course

Fiction
The Designer's Daughter

Get Ready for Book 2 in Lady T's Etiquette Series
100 Modern Day Etiquette Tips
Funeral, Church, Salon, Recreation and much more...

Polish your presence, close business deals, and make a favorable impression everywhere you go. Log on to Lady T's Etiquette Blog at ladytetiquettetips.blogspot.com to find out more.

Books available for bulk sales.

Made in the USA
Charleston, SC
15 February 2013